YO

QUEEN

7 CANDID CONVERSATIONS TO AROUSE THE
CONSCIENCE AND INVOKE A QUEENLY ASCENT.

V.

BY DERRICK J. LITTLE

QUEEN V.

Copyright © 2017 by Derrick J. Little

Printed in USA by Create Space (www.createspace.com)

Author's Contact Information
E-mail Address: Derrickjlittle@gmail.com

More Info.
Blog: Queenvblog.com
Website: www.nowallschristianministry.org

Dedication

I dedicate this book to a phenomenal woman who has had a tremendous impact in my life. To my loving mother, Rosa, I say, thank you for the unconditional love and strength you've shown as a true queen.

Table of Contents

PREFACE

I have always felt a tremendous respect and love for women. Yeah, it's that simple, love is the driving force behind this project. My mother, Rosa, was a true inspiration for this book, her strength and tenacious love for me, and all of my siblings, planted the seeds of love and respect for the women in my life at an early age. I grew up surrounded by strong women, half of whom were single mothers.

There were many days where I witnessed the wisdom, grace, strength and resourcefulness of my mother as she fearlessly raised each of us over the years. She showed me that being a woman takes more than sex appeal; it takes grit, intelligence, character, determination and vision. Queen V. was written to encourage and hopefully inspire thousands of women today to ascribe to those very same characteristics. This book is about self-love, personal accountability and self-development.

We are at a point of unprecedented change at this moment in our generation, and it is my hope that any woman who reads this book will be ready to embrace positive change in her own life. Queen, it is time for you to make your queenly ascent!

ℐNTRODUCTION

For more than nineteen years, I have thought a lot about the topic of self-love, personal accountability, and self-development for women. When I was twenty-one years old, my mother shared something with me that left me stifled for a while. I suppose my father's recent passing at the time prompted her to share something that had been buried in her heart for many years. It was the first time she had let me in on this secret.

According to what my mother told me, shortly after my eldest sister, Kimberly, was born, she began taking birth control pills at the request of my father. She said it was because he did not want to have any more children. My mother says she continued using birth control for some time until she was forced to stop taking it due to an allergic reaction. The pills made her very ill, so it was no longer a viable option for them. My father was a truck driver and a very successful drag racer, so they were frequently on the move.

Three years after Kimberly's birth, my twin brother and I were conceived. Dad wasn't initially happy with the situation, so he insisted that my mother have an abortion. My mother says she considered it for a while, even though she was essentially opposed to that particular notion. Over the first few weeks of her pregnancy, my dad would leave the exact amount needed for the procedure on the kitchen table on his way to work. Then one morning, as he was about to place the money on the table, my mother stopped him and simply stated *"Bill, I am not going to kill my baby (she didn't know she was carrying twins), so if you don't like that, you can go straight to hell!"*

Perhaps, at twenty-one, I was just too young to understand it all. I needed time to gain a clearer perspective on life. Well, I now have that perspective, having lived a bit longer, and having watched the plight of women over the years. What I have seen is what has given me this growing sense of desire to speak out.

Looking back, my twin and I are eternally grateful to our mother for the love and courage it must have taken for her to make that decision. In fact, knowing just how close we came to never being born has caused me to view myself in a totally different light. I am very certain that my life has a special purpose. I don't believe in mere coincidences. I feel everything happens for a reason. What if *you* reading this book is a pure act of God's divine will? For a moment, I want you to consider the notion that maybe I was born to share this message with you. Perhaps you aren't like other women. What if you're supposed to be different?

7

I choose to believe that there is indeed something special about *you* as well as many other women in society today. Every woman is uniquely beautiful and well suited for success. However, it is the quality of her decisions that will either obstruct or enable her to obtain the life, love, and happiness that she truly desires. Choices. That's what it all comes down to.

Unfortunately, some women today aren't making the most of their choices when it comes to their personal lives. Consequently, these women are the ones who will not turn back from their reckless ways of thinking and living. With that said, I am soberly aware that not every woman will shift with this call to conscience. Although, I can't imagine a better time than now to awaken the queens of virtuousness from a slumber of comfortable ignorance.

What I mean by "comfortable ignorance" is that you can decide to be one who considers the pressing issues facing women today and simply choose to ignore the need for real change. You can take the stance that nothing else really matters as long as the very small world around you is not hindered or disturbed. However, I believe that it is time for the collective consciousness of women to be aroused once more to the notion of their own phenomenon. For you, and others like you, it is time to rise above the depreciating norms that society has set for you. I sincerely hope to stir up the greatness within you. I want to challenge you to fearlessly tread a new path for yourself so that with every step, your life will be filled with growth, substance, and divine manifestations!

7 Conversations

AROUSING THE CONSCIENCE AND INVOKING A QUEENLY ASCENT...

1

A CALL TO CONSCIENCE

This might seem strange, but I want to begin our conversation by saying that what concerns me most about some women in our generation is that there seems to be a *hollow* aspect to them. Today's *phenomenal woman* has somehow lost sight of the beauty of her own phenomenon. It seems that for more than a generation the moral consciousness of women has been subjected to extreme opposition. The prism of modern media has had a tremendous impact on how many women choose to see themselves, as well as what it means to be a woman by today's standards. There was once a time when a woman's presumed value was inextricably tied to her moral and feminine honor.

Feminine virtue used to be considered a crown. Today, it is made to appear more like a *ball and chain* around their ankles. Perhaps, there are those who view the idea of virtuousness as something lame or simply outdated. Considering how gradually the bar for women has been lowered in our culture over the past few generations, I can understand how certain corrosive behavior and train of thought has begun to distort the minds of women. Why shouldn't you be proud of your virtuousness?

You Are a Queen!

Embracing your true self and upholding your moral and intellectual integrity should be considered a top priority. Right? I don't think anything about being virtuous is lame or outdated. Embracing virtuousness can change your life! Do you want to know why I am totally against you downplaying your virtuousness? You are a queen! Start *literally* thinking about yourself in that manner. Not just in mere words, but in action! You see, a queen should always have a common touch, but she doesn't have to live in the common places. Her dwelling is in a *high* place where she is seated on a throne. Where she sits bears great significance because it commands blessing, respect, and honor. The crown she wears signifies the *standard* of her inherent power. Keep in mind as well, that a queen's royalty generally *dictates* how she thinks and the way in which she conducts her life's affairs.

Therefore, I encourage you to embrace this queenly *mindset* and to no longer abide by the depreciating norms in today's popular culture. I am not suggesting that you merely adopt a narcissistic attitude, but instead, for you to fearlessly set your life on a *higher* plain. Over the course of this discussion, I hope to arouse your conscience as we touch on certain issues facing women today. Certainly, now is not the time for you to be *afraid* of change. Your personal growth is important. Don't waste time worrying about whether your *crowd* will change, as your life evolves for the better.

In addition, why don't you even begin adjusting your thinking when it comes to men? Become more deliberate in your interactions by not lending yourself emotionally, relationally, or sexually to men of obscure vision, low thinking, and little personal character. Queen, I advise you to take a seat.

Relax, take your time, and don't be in such a hurry when it comes to selecting a possible mate. Instead, make the most of every given opportunity you have, to personally *build yourself up*, and to enrich your quality of life. Moreover, when *you* are ready, men will always be there. Desperation is not a demeanor that is befitting of *royalty*, so hold your peace, and set yourself in a *high* place. Work towards forging the life that you want for yourself. Trust that at the right time, the king you await will make his way up! In the meantime, don't risk getting derailed or distracted by any vain pursuits of men. Besides, if they don't share your values or want the same things in life as you do, why even bother? Seize this moment as an opportunity to change the *quality* of your decisions.

From this day forward, do not *willfully* consent to your own exploitation. I am convinced that if there is to be any significant change concerning this or any other matter in your life it will be because *you* will it.

"Our deepest fear is not that we are inadequate. Our deepest fear is that we are powerful beyond imagination. It is our light more than our darkness, which scares us. We ask ourselves – who are we to be brilliant, beautiful, talented, and fabulous.

But honestly, who are you not to be so? When we liberate ourselves from our own fears, simply our presence may liberate others."

–Marianne Williamson

Queen, there is a power you have over your own life and I hope you will begin to seriously take advantage of it. Get out of your own way! You can't be afraid to be different. Why don't you place a higher premium on yourself by getting comfortable with believing in your own unique brilliance? Furthermore, I urge you to become un-accepting of behaviors or mindsets directed towards you, which contradict the *high* standards you have set for your life. If you can do that, I promise you, it will be extremely liberating. You must believe that you are worth it!

You Are Not a Victim.

I have decided not to berate you, as a woman, by simply making you a hapless victim. You have a mind with which to *think* or do what you will, and so that is why you alone must shoulder the responsibility for *changing* what is unacceptable in your life. Whatever sense of loss you may feel, whether it is in virtue, morality, respectability, value or honor, accept that, for the most part, none of those things can be taken from you; they must be given away. So, stand your ground! Don't allow *anything* to cheapen you when you are the one who is in control.

For instance, in terms of sex, I think women instinctively know that men have little power when it comes to the prospect of sexual intercourse in male and female relationships. Frankly, if a platonic relationship exists between a man and a woman, more than likely, it is platonic because she simply does not want to have sex with the man, instead of visa versa. So, it is my belief that primarily, whether a man engages in a sexual relationship with a woman, is ultimately her call, the same way whether he doesn't is also her call. She essentially has control over the outcome and the same is true for the type of relationship. The significance here is that as a *queen* you must learn to *graciously steward* and *exercise* the virtuous power this affords you. This also speaks to the notion of discipline and self-restraint you must learn to exercise.

The Choice Is Yours

Your discipline must always outweigh your desire. Why? Well, because your health and quality of life are just that important. As I alluded to earlier, make the most of *your* precious time. Why not shift more of your attention towards your own personal *development* and *giftedness*? Be wise so that there will be little time for distractions. As you remain focused on self-growth and building the life you want, perhaps, you will find yourself making better decisions. Remember, *only you* have the power to determine whether the choices you make will be made in accordance with the low standards of society, or from a *higher* moral and intellectual standard.

Hey, being a *queen* isn't about doing what is expedient or comfortable, but some woman must be willing to take such a stance! I say that because considering the cultural climate we live in, I am fully aware that what I am suggesting isn't *popular*, but it will set you apart from the *commoners* who will not change course. They will watch your queenly ascent. Others will see in you a patient, secure, dignified demeanor the likes of which hasn't been seen in more than a generation. Take charge of your life, virtuous queen, and break away from the pack! Dare to be different and to *personify* a more excellent way of living! Again, those who choose to embrace disrespect, self-hatred and insecurity will all watch as your life begets respect, honor, and commanded blessings!

The Pulse of Today

Simply put, the choice is yours! Therefore, from this point on I will try to paint a clear picture of some specific things *you* have the power to change. As the Jedi would say, "the force is strong with you." Remember this as we venture on and I hope that you will see how impactful your life can be just by making better decisions. Amidst all the *smoke* and *mirrors* today, maybe it's time for you to stop and take a careful look at something. Each day in America, 2,494 babies are born to mothers, *who are not high school graduates*, 2,411 babies are born into poverty, and 400,000 babies are born each year to teenaged mothers.

At this point, does it matter whether you are reading this as a teen, college student, young professional or even an older woman? These issues are affecting women today everywhere and in all age groups and educational brackets. What are *you* going to do to change this trend? Furthermore, it is a desperate time in our generation when an estimated 2.5 million *grandparents* are forced to raise grandchildren without adequate help from their natural parents. I suggest that it is time to no longer accept the *unacceptable* when each year in America approximately 1.2 million abortions take place; and of which 85% are performed on unmarried women according to recent statistics taken by the center for disease control.

The Moral Conscience

On average, there's said to be at least three reasons why some women choose to have an abortion. There are those who say that having a baby would interfere with work, school, or other responsibilities. While, others say that they cannot afford a child and insist that they don't want to be single mothers. So, there you have it, no *smoke*, and no *mirrors!* Take a hard look at what the *real world* around you, looks like for many women today.

I am aware that change won't happen in a day, but don't you think it is worth it to do some things differently? Besides, it has been stated: *"Only a fool does the same thing, but expects different results."*

As I consider the distressing signs of our time the most compelling truth is that today's phenomenal woman must emerge! She must free herself from the clutches of fear, insecurity, self-hatred, and comfortable ignorance, in order to save not only her own life, but that of future generations. My objective isn't to arouse offense, but to respectfully make a plea to your conscience.

I have always held the view that behind the demise of any great civilization you will find the decay of its' moral and social standards. Well, in a hypothetical sense, I feel that women represent a type of *"moral consciousness"* in society which can potentially lend its influence to the entire atmosphere of a nation.

Surely, this great *value* women hold can *never* be overlooked or overstated. As kids, they are our nurturers and teachers. Even scripture bears witness as it reminds us: *"For as woman came from man, even so man also comes through woman."* That is right, for more than nine months, women are given the *privilege* of carrying in their wombs the very lives of generations! In my opinion, that alone makes *you* too important to remain ignorant of the significance your life carries! There is so much creativeness and gifting that's been invested in you. Even now, percolating on the inside of you are business ideas, inventions, concepts, as well as many other things that must come to fruition.

With Great Power Comes Great Responsibility

That's why later, we're going to talk about the *planting of destiny*. It is important for you to get in touch with how *valuable* and powerful your *contribution* to the world is. It has been said: *"With great power comes great responsibility."* Well, I want you to know that, as a woman, the same is true with you. You are an anointed queen and so there must be the necessary adjustments made to your lifestyle as it aligns itself with this reality.

Sex Cannot Be Your Best Asset

Sexual promiscuity is a very prevalent thing in every culture, but that doesn't make it responsible. Can you believe that, today, your personal status can depend on the person you choose to have sex with? In fact, many people derive great self-worth out of having random sex. This is unfortunate. There should be so much more to you and what you have to offer, than just sex.

Some women nowadays *allow* themselves to become objects of utter exploitation. In fact, there are even some who hold fast to the notion of there being such a great disparity among suitable men in society today.

Who's feeding women such an erroneous notion? Sure, there are plenty of suitable men out here in society. Perhaps, there is a real need for greater maturity among men. I'll give you that, but rest assured that men aren't on the verge of mass extinction! Just take the time to choose wisely. Don't be foolish enough to consider *sex* as a viable option for finding a mate. I am not trying to be condescending towards anyone; it's just that I feel this perception seems to be generally leading many women astray. Specifically, when a woman uses sex as her most alluring asset, it is like parading a school of seals before a ferocious killer whale.

Sex Only Signals a Feast

Ultimately, more times than not, what that does is it brings all of the *predators* out; and they are not looking for a wife. Wake up! They're mainly interested in a feast! It really doesn't matter if you're being *"wined and dined"* because if sex is your best means to getting that sort of treatment, sadly you've already been exploited!

Hey, here's a notion that I need you to get really comfortable with: *"you aren't just some consolation prize for a few chips and dip! You are a queen, whose worth is simply immeasurable."* Stop playing yourself, because after the frivolous games are done, all you'll have are a few *cheap thrills* to go along with a face full of shame. You're so much better than that! Sex can't be the best thing you have to offer, nor can you *allow* it to become an *addiction* that drives an *unhealthy* lifestyle.

Remember what we sampled earlier as a pulse in today's culture. There's just too much at stake considering the present epidemic of abortion, teen pregnancy, and poverty, facing our era. Even consider that some single parent homes may be attributed to the type of irrational, erratic, and reckless attitude that exist among many in our culture. As a woman, you simply can't afford to be *undisciplined* with your life. Don't you think so?

Discipline Must Outweigh Desire

I stated earlier that, *"Your discipline must outweigh your desire."* Why is that important? Well, what do you want out of life? What type of person do you want to be known as? What goals are you actively pursuing? Do you want to be *happily* married? Do you want to be a mother someday? Are you content in your singleness? These are just a few of the possible reasons why it should matter. At this moment in your life, no matter where you are, I urge you to allow *discipline* to outweigh desire. Perception is everything, yet, for many, the problem is that we tend to *"put the cart before the horse."*

Predominantly, most people place sex ahead of marriage, intimacy before relationship, and desire before the notion of rational self-discipline. The premise here is that *without* self-discipline, no matter what you want in life, success will be impossible. Perhaps the greatest hindrance in most of our lives is that we tend to show little self-restraint.

Who knows, maybe we have grown to like it. To love chaos and dysfunction is to truly *promote* our own extinction. When there is utter *disregard* for what is right, everything becomes subject to distortion. In any case, today, I think this is the precise reason why you should take a different approach to sex and even relationships.

Be Open to A Different View

Nowadays, when it comes to our common perception of sex and relationships, there must be a true willingness for meaningful dialogue and growth. The common perceptions of both are badly misconstrued, and so men and women alike must be open to the idea of a new approach regarding each.

For the moment, I want us to simply focus on the foundational premise for each. Intimacy is the *common* factor in both relationships and sex. It is the foundational basis of any type of relationship because, in a natural sense, intimacy is a process that tends to *promote* careful understanding, tenderness, closeness, and familiarity. In essence, intimacy should *produce* a more mature, *healthy* relationship. This is where some of the greatest misconceptions evolve. Sex is in fact a form of intimacy, but it alone does not constitute the full concept. Perhaps this is a good reason why dating these days just isn't as successful for many. How can we really get to know someone if we don't allow ourselves time to *"develop"* a careful understanding for, or a familiarity with, that particular person?

Relationship alone does not beget Intimacy

Intimacy requires the *investment* of time and self if there's to be any meaningful relationship. Contrary to popular belief, just because you are in a relationship doesn't necessarily *guarantee* the development of intimacy. If that were the case, then there would be many more healthy relationships, marriages, and families today.

Generally, that's where many go wrong, by not taking the time to get to know people. We typically don't allow the careful *development* of intimacy to *qualify* the nature of our relationships. Not every relationship is supposed to be marital or even sexual. Some may naturally evolve into friendships, while many others will simply remain platonic in nature.

Yet, regardless of their standing, each should require the investment of time and careful understanding. One simply should not avoid the necessary process of gaining a common familiarity with people. Say, for instance, you were going to need a major surgery, wouldn't you want to become as *familiar* as possible with the physician? If you needed to find a childcare provider, would you just *haphazardly* hire anyone? No, I suspect there would be a very careful selection process. Well, that same type of *thoughtful* and *discerning* manner should manifest itself when it comes to how you enter into *any* type of relationship.

Stop Misappropriating Sex

As we've already discussed, sex is greatly abused in our culture mainly due to its misappropriation. For some, sex is a weapon or perhaps a bargaining chip to get what they want. While in essence, it should be a tool used to *build* families, and to further enrich the intimate *bonds* of marriage. This is why I believe that the *careful understanding* and *development* of intimacy should qualify both the persons and the relationship, while sex only helps to enrich and *reaffirm* that committed bond. Sex is a good thing, that's how it was always intended to be.

However, as Dr. Myles Monroe once stated: *"If you don't know the purpose of a thing you will abuse it."* I agree with that notion, considering how different forms of reckless abuse drives most of life's calamities. Don't allow your life to be driven by recklessness! Take the time to get comfortable with yourself. Then when the right opportunity presents itself, hopefully you will find yourself developing a closeness and familiarity with the *best* man. Trust me, if you allow time for this to happen, then your relationships will become more meaningful. I also believe sex can be even more enjoyable when it is shared with the man who has *qualified* himself by a *sacred* promise… He puts a ring on it!

A Call to Conscience

How did you feel about this conversation?

_____
_____
_____
_____
_____
_____

*What are some personal things you took from this conversation?

_____
_____
_____
_____

*Do you have any personal experiences you are comfortable talking about?

_____
_____
_____
_____
_____

*WHAT 10 QUEENS ARE YOU GOING TO SHARE THIS CONVERSATION WITH?

1._____ 6._____
2._____ 7._____
3._____ 8._____
4._____ 9._____
5._____ 10._____

BY THE WAY, HERE ARE SOME TALKING POINTS...

Feminine Virtue Is a Crown!

-Embrace a Queenly mindset.

-Lose the desperation.

-Refocus on the phenomenon that is you.

_____

Ascend to Your High Place!

-Become a visionary!

-Raise your standard.

2

SCARED OF BEAUTIFUL

Ms. I want to begin this conversation with a simple question.

Who are you? Think about that for a moment. Now I would like you to take a second to write down your answer.

_____

_____

_____

Why is that so important? Well, because whatever you've written down is the most telling factor about how you not only view yourself, but also how others perceive you. The question of self-identification is perhaps the most fundamental issue of your life. When you were born, it is certain that you came wrapped in raw, unfettered destiny. With that said, I believe you possess an identity that's uniquely yours. In fact, why don't you consider what makes you different from everyone else? It's ok if at first you are uncertain about how to respond. Take your time, perhaps you've never really looked within yourself to answer the question: "What makes you unique?" Really, isn't that where *self-love* begins, at the point of your own self-reflection? How you see yourself is tremendously important because if you allow *others* to interpret your self-image who can say whether you will like what you see?

Face Off

Can I ask you another serious question? Who or what is defining your self-image? I wonder whether the persona you carry today truly represents who you are, or if it is just a shallow portrayal of someone else you would rather be? Only *you* know the truth. This sort of notion isn't too far-fetched, since it appears to have become the norm these days. There are those of us who are not happy with ourselves or the lives we are currently living.

As such, there is a tendency for us to simply *abandon* our own selves, taking on another person's persona as a result.

Who are you trying to be like anyway? Is it Beyoncé, Jennifer Aniston, Taylor Swift, Rihanna, and Angelina? If you are married, whose marriage are you trying to model yours after, if not your own? Whose life do you desire to imitate? Open your eyes! Tell me what you see because whatever is superficial or unauthentic, only you can change it. Furthermore, today there are hosts of modern mediums operating within our society that I believe help to distort your identity and plague your way of thinking. The key to overcoming many of them is by again, *you* first becoming comfortable with the light of your own beautiful reflection. For a moment, I would like you to say this to yourself. *"I am simply beautiful!"*

Now realize that I didn't ask you to say it because you needed to be reminded, I did so because *often,* what seems to get lost as we attempt to redefine ourselves is this: we were *already* wonderful in the first place! Many people aren't quite convinced of that, and so they try too hard. Generally, they tend to *overcompensate,* which only makes things that much worse. I want you to consider the following words...

"You alone created my inner being. You knitted me together inside my mother. I will give thanks to you because I have been so amazingly and miraculously made. Your works are miraculous, and my soul is fully aware of this. My bones were not hidden from you when I was being made in secret, when I was being skillfully woven in an underground workshop. Your eyes saw me when I was only a fetus. Every day [of my life] was recorded in your book before one of them had taken place." - **Psalm 139: 13-16**

Hey, why don't you get *comfortable* with your own unique beauty? Queen, there is something (about you) that you must *believe* far more than anyone else does. You are truly phenomenal, and that's just how it is! There's no explanation needed, no apology is necessary. Accept the fact that you were simply *created* to be beautiful! Now here's the only problem with all of that. Do *you* believe it? In fact, that is possibly the main reason why many women suffer with their self-image. They don't believe in their own beauty.

Who told you that?

Today there are those who have totally bought into certain factions of the media, entertainment, and fashion industries, which promote stereotypes and impressions that totally undermines their true moral, intellectual, and feminine value as virtuous women.

I don't care what you've heard or seen modeled on a runway!

Keep this in mind: *"Anything that shapes your perspective also has the power to influence your character."*

Certainly, you have the right to live and conduct your life as you please. However, I challenge you to no longer accept the unacceptable. Realize that it is not acceptable for you to allow BET, MTV, Cosmopolitan, Elle, Vogue, Allure, Ebony, Essence, or any other form of mass media to define who you are.

My point here is not to *demonize* entertainment and the media, but to suggest that it all has a self-serving *agenda* worth paying closer attention to. Essentially, BET, MTV, Cosmopolitan, Elle, Vogue, Allure, Ebony, Essence etc. all want *to plant images* in your mind; they want to sell you their products! Therefore, *subconsciously*, what the system of mass media does is to constantly define and redefine who you are, and how you see yourself. That's how they make their millions! Once you buy into the system, whether you know it or not, it immediately begins to meticulously eat away at your *self-perception*.

Once that happens, it's not long before you are swept away by the currents of covetousness, insecurity, and *inauthentic* redefinition. We live during a time where image and social status has never meant more. So the real question is, just how much of yourself are you willing to give up in hopes of achieving the status quo? How you see yourself is what matters, since you know yourself better than anyone else does. So, choose to love how wonderful you are!

Running Scared

The media prompts women to run from themselves in order to achieve what it projects as true beauty and *accepted* sex appeal. Victoria Secret, particularly, does a masterful job of selling sexy. Certainly, the genius there is in how it plays to "the secret enemies" lurking in the mind of the average woman who looks nothing like the young sex goddesses scantily displayed in their brilliant ads. What they are selling isn't really that much of a secret at all. I think those types of advertisements subtly appeal to the darker side of most women. Again, this is only my opinion, but that type of pandering not only sells millions of dollars of merchandise; it also does its part in stoking the flames of insecurity and self-hatred among women of all ages. Why don't you just think about that for a moment? Can you imagine the average adolescent female today, as they scour every major fashion magazine for the latest trends?

Subconsciously, they look to television and other forms of media for self-definition. Essentially, they get "lost in translation," as they attempt to find some sort of identity for themselves. So how do you think all of this is working out for them? Well, it seems only natural that constant exposure to these *thin-ideal* media and magazine images, consequently increases body dissatisfaction, negative mood states, decreased self-esteem, and even eating disorders among many of today's young women. Then guess what else? Some of these very same girls are growing up as incubators of insecurity, carrying around in them a growing hatred of themselves. Why? Oh, I guess you can say that's the price of beauty, but I dare to ask the simple question: "Whose beauty?" Cause' to me it sure isn't the God forged image of themselves that they're constantly trying to achieve, or become at ease with.

Sleeping Beauty

Let me be fair in saying that the media and entertainment industries aren't solely responsible for the issues women face. At some point, I think *you,* as an individual, must also take a greater sense of personal responsibility. Certainly, those industries are going to do what they're good at, "selling," so the onus then falls squarely to you as to whether you will *buy into* what they're selling.

I know that self-image is important. I see nothing wrong with being trendy or fashionable, just don't let it define you. I'm not personally calling for the boycotting of any of today's magazines, but I am encouraging you not to allow them to define the way you think about yourself. I truly believe that over-consumption [psychological] of the media and the views it portrays can be extremely dangerous.

So again, let me state the obvious: BET, MTV, Cosmopolitan, Elle, Vogue, Allure, Essence etc. all want *to plant images* in your mind.

There's an old saying that goes: *"If you want something done right you have to do it yourself."* Well, it's time for you to stop accepting the unacceptable. My firm belief is that many of

In a sense, ***"we're all products of the media machine."*** So, constantly, it has to subtly define and redefine how we see ourselves. It is how the entire industry makes millions! Just food for thought.

the challenges women face will never evolve for the better until *you* become the greatest components of that evolution. Notice that from 1848, at the Seneca Falls Woman's Rights Convention, until the year 1920, when women finally won the right to vote, where there was *significant* change, *women* were the biggest proponents of it. I sincerely believe in your ability to *change* the world around you. Therefore, I strongly suggest that if you want to see change, be prepared to *change* with it.

Change You Can Believe In

Just for a moment, I want you to seriously consider everything that you hate about being a woman in today's secular society. Think about the sexism, sexual exploitation, abortion, early teen pregnancy, single parent homes (mostly women), economic inequality, relationships (finding a good man), etc. Do you really know that you have the power to truly transform your own world?

It's about *owning the change you want* and staking it all on what *you* are willing to do differently. Today, there seem to be too many followers and not enough of those who are

"If you really want change, then you must be willing to make a change."

willing to break from the pack. Are you one of the "leading ladies" who is ready to seize the change she wants in her life? Good! Now the first thing you must do is make the decision to no longer allow others to define you. I guess what I want to do is invoke in you the same spirit of intolerance, dissatisfaction and change which aroused even those great "leading women" of the not so distant past. Surely, now is the time for you to begin decisively stamping out every thought of self-hate, doubt, and insecurity! Therefore, moving forward in the spirit of revival and civil protest to the status quo, allow me to further propagate the following thoughts...

Phenomenal Woman

"Pretty women wonder where my secret lies. I'm not cute or built to suit a fashion model's size, but when I start to tell them, they think I'm telling lies. I say, it's in the reach of my arms the span of my hips, the stride of my step, the curl of my lips. I'm a woman phenomenally. Phenomenal woman, that's me.

I walk into a room just as cool as you please, and to a man, the fellows stand or fall down on their knees. Then they swarm around me, a hive of honeybees. I say, it's the fire in my eyes, and the flash of my teeth, the swing in my waist, and the joy in my feet.

I'm a woman phenomenally. Phenomenal woman, that's me. Men themselves have wondered what they see in me. They try so much, but they can't touch my inner mystery.

When I try to show them they say they still can't see. I say, it's in the arch of my back, the sun of my smile, the ride of my breasts, the grace of my style. I'm a woman phenomenally. Phenomenal woman, that's me. Now you understand just why my head's not bowed. I don't shout or jump about or have to talk real loud.

When you see me passing it ought to make you proud. I say it's in the click of my heels, the bend of my hair, the palm of my hand, the need of my care, 'cause I'm a woman phenomenally. Phenomenal woman, that's me." - Maya Angelou

Why don't you meditate on those words? Internalize them, as you too are phenomenal as any! Let Maya Angelou's poetic depiction be an example to you. In this day, let there arise in the heart of every woman, such a notion, such a spirit, which so boldly embraces the value of her true self-worth! I urge you to begin divesting of every conception of your sexuality and feminine beauty, as it is being interpreted, in most of the TV media, fashion and entertainment industries. Frankly, I think it's time for *you* to look in the mirror and begin to really deal with yourself! Go ahead; make peace with who you really are beyond the makeup, earrings, designer clothing, and the status quo. Get comfortable with you! Stop leaving yourself so available for another's definition. The million-dollar question is how you see yourself. Perhaps that's the real issue because as we've discussed earlier:

"Anything that shapes your perspective, also has the power to influence your character."

In essence, we all come into this world as unique tapestries. Each of us are made according to God's own distinct, tasteful interpretation. Once more, a fact worth noting is that you were born beautiful! Don't be held in subjection to someone else's "reinterpretation." Remember, you're a heavenly masterpiece!

There is a saying: *"People can only go as far as you allow them to."* Unfortunately, you don't control everything that is said or done in society, but you do reserve the right to decide how you will respond. Decide to take back the right to your own self-definition, because it's something far too valuable to leave in the care of others. Don't you think so? Personally, in your life experiences have you ever heard or even said to someone: *"I think he or she's a nice person, but only if they were just a bit more..."* Do yourself a favor by steering clear of those types of statements, and of the people who make them. Why? Well, because they tend to be influenced by unrealistic expectations. Both are prospects that could lead you down a path to self-hatred and life-altering decisions. Be very careful with your life, because before long you could find yourself acting, speaking, and doing things you never thought you would.

Ok, now at this moment, we are going to *shift* a little as I feel there is something more for us to explore in our conversation. As I alluded to earlier, many women battle "secret enemies" in their daily lives. At this point, we are going to delve into the wilderness of your own personal behavior and sometimes-murky thought life because, what you think or say about yourself can be just as detrimental to your mental, physical, and emotional health as anything else can. In most cases, you really are what you think.

Section Two

Check Your Thoughts
And Watch Your Mouth!

Sticks, Stones, and Words

Have you ever heard this phrase, "Sticks and stones may break my bones, but words can never harm me"? The reality is that words *do* matter, and in many instances, can be more critically damaging than any stick or rock. As a matter of fact, if you've ever been hit by the right words, you can hardly tell the difference. I guess what I am getting at is that even beyond other people's definitions, we still have to be careful about how we define ourselves. How many times in your life have you said something totally self-deprecating about yourself? Perhaps it was your hair, teeth, or clothing. Whatever it was, you just weren't happy with something about yourself.

Surely, we've all done this at some point, which is fine; although when it becomes a habitual occurrence, then there needs to be some serious self-examination. How often do you find yourself being bombarded by the harshest of criticisms? Has there been a time in your life when you were afflicted by the most sinister of words, yet the biggest problem was that they were actually coming out of your own mouth? If that's how you roll, then please ease up and give yourself a break from this type of unhealthy self-mutilation!

You know, it was a little challenging preparing to write this book, simply because the more aware I became of some of the issues women face today, the angrier it made me. While doing my research, I came across a compelling survey on Glamour.com. The survey was quite disturbing and made me think, *"something has to be done about this! Every woman in the world needs to see this survey."* Read these words: *"You are a fat, worthless pig." "You're too thin. No man is ever going to want you." "Ugly. Big. Gross."*

Are these horrifying comments on some awful website or just the rant of an abusive, controlling boyfriend? No, shockingly, these are the actual words many *women* are saying to *themselves* on any typical day. For some, such thoughts are fleeting, but for others, this dialogue plays on a constant punishing loop, according to a new exclusive

"A man's stomach shall be satisfied from the fruit of his mouth; from the produce of his lips he shall be filled. Death and life are in the power of the tongue and those who love it will eat its fruit."
– Proverbs 18:20, 21

Glamour survey of more than 300 women of all sizes. Its research found that, on average, women have 13 negative thoughts about their bodies daily—nearly one for every waking hour.

And a disturbing number of women confessed to having 35, 50 or even 100 hateful thoughts about their own shapes each day.

The experiment asked women cross the country to note every negative or anxious thought they had about their bodies over the course of one full day. The results were shocking: A whopping *97 percent* admitted to having at least one "I hate my body" moment.

When Is Self-Hatred Ever Acceptable?

"That is *a lot*, yet I'm not totally surprised," says Ann Kearney-Cooke, Ph.D., a Cincinnati psychologist who specializes in body image and helped *Glamour* design their survey. "It's become such an accepted norm to put yourself down that if someone says she likes her body, she's the odd woman out.

I was in a group discussion recently, and when one woman said, 'I actually feel OK about the way I look,' another woman scrunched up her face and said, 'I have never in my whole life heard anyone say that—and I'm not sure I even believe you.' That's how pervasive this negative body talk is. It's actually more acceptable to insult your body than to praise it." And we seem to be well aware of how hard we are on ourselves.

Nearly 63 percent of Glamour's survey respondents said they had roughly the same number of negative thoughts as they expected. But few realized how venomous those thoughts were until they were down on paper. So how has this become OK? "Our unattainable cultural beauty ideals, our celebrity worship, those all play a part," says Kearney-Cooke. But another big reason is that we've actually *trained* ourselves to be this way.

What's on Your Mind?

"Neuroscience has shown that whatever you focus on shapes your brain. If you're constantly thinking negative thoughts about your body, that neural pathway becomes stronger and those thoughts become habitual," Kearney-Cooke explains. "Imagine a concert pianist. Her brain would have stronger neural pathways that support musicality and dexterity than someone who hadn't spent her life practicing." Our "training" begins early. In a University of Central Florida study of three to six-year-old girls, nearly half of them were already worried about being fat, and roughly a third said they wanted to change something about their body.

"There are only so many times you can be hit with the message that your body isn't 'right' whether you see it on TV, hear it from your mom, or just feel it in the ether—before you internalize it and start beating yourself up for not being as perfect as you 'should' be," says Nichole Wood-Barcalow, Ph.D., a psychologist at the Laureate Eating Disorders Program in Tulsa, Oklahoma. As Maureen Dorsett, 28, of Washington, D.C., who counted 11 negative thoughts the day she did this experiment, puts it: "I always saw my negative thoughts as a way of improving myself, of calling attention to what I need to work on.

Stop the Negative Talk

"If a guy said to me, 'Wow, your belly looks flabby today,' that would be really offensive. Somehow, these thoughts never seemed as degrading coming from my own mind. Maybe I had just gotten so used to having them." To make matters worse, negative talk has become part of the way women bond. "Friends getting together and tearing themselves down is such a common thing that it's hard to avoid," says Kearney-Cooke. The chatter happens on Facebook and among coworkers, and is broadcast with surprising viciousness on shows like *Real Housewives* and *Bridalplasty (on which one perfectly cute contestant declared, "I want this butt face fixed!")* And all that public bashing makes the internal insults seem normal. As one woman said: "When others make comments about their bodies, it makes me think about *mine* more."

Hmm. If our brains are virtually wired this way—and outside cultural forces aren't helping—how can one stop the self-hate? They were determined to find out. When *Glamour* analyzed the data to look for a cause of these ruthless thoughts, a fascinating trend emerged: Respondents who were unsatisfied with their career or relationship tended to report more negative body thoughts than women who were content in those areas.

Why Your Body May Not be the Problem

What's more, feeling uncomfortable emotions of any sort— stress, loneliness, even boredom—made many women start berating their looks. "If we're having a bad day, we often take those negative emotions out on our body, rather than directing them at what's really troubling us, like our boss or boyfriend," says Wood-Barcalow. In fact—and this part's important—whether you're unhappy in general is a much larger factor in how you feel about your body than what your body actually *looks* like.

In *Glamour's* survey, thin and average-weight women were just as likely to insult themselves as overweight ones. As Wood-Barcalow recites to her patients: "It's all about your body—and absolutely nothing about your body."

Consider this? "Let's say you're in a meeting and you suddenly think, Eww, my arms are huge," says Kearney-Cooke. "Well, you've had those same arms all day. Why are you suddenly feeling bad about them now? Maybe it's because you don't think your professional ideas are being valued or you're not fulfilled in your job. Instead of focusing on the real issue, all you can think of is hating your arms. And it becomes a vicious cycle: All the push-ups in the world won't make you feel better, because your arms weren't the problem to begin with."

Silencing Your Inner (Mean Girl)

So how can you muzzle that insulting internal voice and get on with your life? "I'm way too hard on myself, but I don't know how to lessen my negative thoughts," admits Rebecca Illson, 25, of Birmingham, Michigan, who counted negative thoughts over the course of the day. That age-old advice to "love your body" is—let's be honest—trite and unhelpful. "It's not about achieving a 'perfect' body image. That's not realistic," says Wood-Barcalow. "Even the most confident women have doubts. But they've learned to combat those thoughts rather than allow them to take over."

It's worth it for not just the mental peace, but your *physical* health as well. Research at the University of British Columbia, Vancouver, suggests that women who obsess over their body and diet have chronically elevated levels of the stress hormone cortisol (even when their life is *not* otherwise stressed)—and, as a result, may suffer from elevated blood pressure, lower bone density, higher amounts of unhealthy belly fat and even menstrual problems. "And this was among women in their twenties!" exclaims lead researcher Jennifer Bedford, Ph.D. "If you continue on this path, it could have a real impact on heart, bone and reproductive health 10 or 20 years down the road."

Hope for Real Change

Well my friend, how did you feel about the survey? Hopefully, it touched you on a very real level since ultimately *you* alone have control over what you say and think about yourself. Remember, you may be victimized by anyone or anything, but that doesn't mean you have to become a victim. I certainly don't want you to go away from this intellectual experience feeling as if the world owes you an apology. If I have successfully communicated the message I intended, you should be simmering with a greater sense of self-appreciation. I hope you see yourself differently and have a greater love for the beautiful person that you are.

My deliberate intent is to inspire a deeper desire for change in your life. Therefore, as we move forward, let me say that the real hope for any meaningful change concerning today's issues affecting women, really begins with you. That's right, your decisions going forward are important, and they can drastically transform your overall quality of life. Don't let anyone mislead you any longer, because sister, there is *power* in feminine virtuousness! The journey has only just begun for you and me. There is so much more for us to touch on. Come now, and let us keep this "V" train moving!

Scared of Beautiful

How did you feel about this conversation?

_____

_____

_____

_____

_____

_____

*What are some personal things you took from this conversation?

_____

_____

_____

_____

*Do you have any personal experiences you are comfortable talking about?

_____

_____

_____

_____

*WHAT 8 QUEENS ARE YOU GOING TO SHARE THIS CONVERSATION WITH?

1._____   6._____
2._____   7._____
3._____   8._____

BY THE WAY, HERE ARE SOME TALKING POINTS...

GET COMFORTABLE WITH YOUR OWN UNIQUE BEAUTY.

-*How is your self-image?*

-*Rid yourself of other people's interpretation of worth and beauty*

-*Are you being authentically "you?"*

-*Stop hating the good more than the bad!*

CHECK YOUR THOUGHTS AND WATCH YOUR MOUTH!

-*Reign in those toxic thoughts!*

-*How do you monitor your words?*

-*Stop the "negative" body talk!*

IF YOU REALLY WANT CHANGE, THEN BE WILLING TO MAKE A CHANGE.

-*What are you allowing to shape your perspective!*

-*Are you willing to change your behavior?*

-*Watch the perspectives you choose to buy into.*

3

THE REAL QUESTIONS

Alrighty then, we've come to a new stage in our dialogue. At this point, I want to pose to you a few questions that I believe are truly beneficial to the overall quality of your lifestyle. Don't you think it's time to start asking *yourself* the right questions? Ultimately, I am not in the least bit intrigued by the questions *you should ask a man*, but rather in what you should be asking yourself. How often do you take the time to really think about your life or the type of choices you are making? Do you believe, as it is often stated: *"we are the sum of our thoughts?"* If that's the case, then perhaps you must start thinking differently about a lot of things, mainly about yourself.

To be or not to be, that is the question! –It really doesn't matter how you were raised or what other women in your bloodline have done before you. What certainly matters *now* is what *you* decide to do with your life experience. Truly, I think it all begins with whether you elect to answer the right questions.

The First Question:

What sort of character do I have?

_____
_____
_____
_____

*What does "character" mean to me?

_____
_____
_____
_____

*How is my character shaping my quality of life?

_____
_____
_____
_____
_____

*What am I going to do differently?

1._____ 4._____
2._____ 5._____
3._____ 6._____

THE SECOND QUESTION:
AM I LIVING AS MY AUTHENTIC SELF?

_____
_____
_____
_____

*WHAT DO I NOT LIKE ABOUT ME?

_____
_____
_____
_____

*WHOSE PERSONA HAVE I ADOPTED AS MORE ACCEPTABLE THAN MY OWN? WHO AM I TRYING TO IMITATE?

_____
_____
_____

*WHAT ARE SOME THINGS I LIKE ABOUT MYSELF?

1._____   6._____
2._____   7._____
3._____   8._____
4._____   9._____
5._____   10._____

THE THIRD QUESTION:

HOW IS MY QUALITY OF LIFE?

_____

_____

_____

_____

*AM I LIVING THE LIFE THAT I WANT TO LIVE?

*WHAT HOPE DO I HAVE FOR MY FUTURE?

_____

_____

_____

_____

*HOW DO I BEGIN TO LIVE THE LIFE I WANT?

1._____   6._____
2._____   7._____
3._____   8._____
4._____   9._____
5._____   10._____

THE FOURTH QUESTION:

WHAT VISION DO I HAVE FOR MY LIFE?

_____
_____
_____

*WHAT ARE MY SHORT-TERM GOALS?

_____
_____
_____
_____
_____
_____

*WHAT ARE MY LONG-TERM GOALS?

_____
_____
_____
_____
_____
_____

*WHAT ARE ANY POSSIBLE HINDRANCES?

1._____ 6._____
2._____ 7._____
3._____ 8._____
4._____ 9._____
5._____ 10._____

THE FIFTH QUESTION:

WHAT DO I FILL MY MIND WITH DAILY?

_____
_____

52

*AM I AWARE OF MY THOUGHTS ABOUT MY LIFE AND MYSELF?

_____
_____
_____

*WHAT ARE SOME OF THOSE THOUGHTS?

_____
_____
_____

*WHAT IS THE STATE OF MY MENTAL AND EMOTIONAL HEALTH?

_____
_____
_____

*WHAT ARE (8) SOURCES OF POSITIVE REINFORCEMENT FOR YOUR LIFE?

1._____   5._____
2._____   6._____
3._____   7._____
4._____   8._____

THE SIXTH QUESTION:

HOW PEACEFUL IS MY LIFE?

_____
_____
_____

*HOW AM I DEALING WITH STRESS?

_____
_____
_____

*WHAT FACIAL EXPRESSIONS DO I ROUTINELY WEAR? HOW CAN I BEGIN TO SMILE MORE?

_____
_____
_____

*WHAT ACTIVITIES GIVE YOU THE MOST PEACE OF MIND?

1._____   6._____
2._____   7._____
3._____   8._____
4._____   9._____
5._____   10._____

THE SEVENTH QUESTION:

HOW IS MY SPIRITUAL CONNECTION WITH GOD?

_____
_____
_____

*IS THIS TYPE OF LIFESTYLE IMPORTANT TO ME?

_____
_____
_____

54

*HOW DO I BUILD MY SPIRITUAL SELF?

_____

_____

_____

_____

*WHAT DO I BELIEVE NEEDS TO CHANGE ABOUT MY LIFE?

1._____ 6._____
2._____ 7._____
3._____ 8._____
4._____ 9._____
5._____ 10._____

THE EIGHTH QUESTION:

HOW ARE MY RELATIONSHIPS?

_____

_____

_____

*HOW ARE MY RELATIONSHIPS WITH MY PARENTS,
SIBLINGS, AND FRIENDS? ARE THESE BONDS STRONG?

_____

_____

_____

_____

*WHAT TYPE OF RELATIONAL BAGGAGE AM I CARRYING?

_____
_____
_____
_____

*HOW IS IT AFFECTING ME ON A PERSONAL AND
EMOTIONAL LEVEL?

_____
_____
_____

4

THE STANDARD OF

VIRTUOUSNESS

"Who can find a virtuous woman? For her worth is far more valuable than rubies. The heart of her husband is so secure that he has no need for any other treasure." - Proverbs 31:10, 11

What is virtuousness? In my opinion, it is the *purest* essence of the feminine psyche. Furthermore, it is an attitude of regality, which embodies confidence and grace; it is the *uncompromising* standard which reflects a woman's moral and intellectual state of being. This is what some would call a "constant" not a variable. Virtuousness is no different to a woman than her hands, feet, nose or mouth, it's the part of her identity that should never change.

A woman's virtuousness is the *undercurrent* in her life, which should temper *every* facet. Self-image, self-worth, self-government, moral character, love, relationships, family, business, everything that encompasses her life should be marked by it. This is not just a simple gimmick or some slick play on words. It is what it is, and so I hope your interest is peaked because we're going deeper.

That Wonderful Feeling

Now that you have been introduced to the existence of the concept of virtuousness I want to ask a question. Have you ever noticed any trace of it in your own life? Perhaps you have, but just weren't aware that it should be embraced as a part of you. Think about the natural demeanor of a little girl? Most are unconsciously consumed with just how "wonderful" they are. It is a wonderful feeling they have about themselves that wasn't captured from any magazine, television show, or movie. As it would appear, they are *born* that way. Personally, I have seven other siblings, four of whom are sisters. I can remember how, as children, my twin brother and I would play outside. We built sand castles, climbed trees, and sometimes we even wanted our sisters to join us during certain adventures; but they would say "no we don't want to do that cause' we're girls!"

Can't you just hear the sheer vanity? Oh well, I guess they just couldn't see the triumph in building the palace of "Camelot," considering the delicate slosh of their silly mud pies. Perhaps, while we were consumed with achieving feats of bravery and adventure, they felt too "wonderful" to participate. Psssss. Have you ever had that feeling? Surely, you have!

I Am a Lady

Are you familiar with Martin Lawrence's comedic characterization of a woman named "Sheneneh?" As outrageous as she could be, there was still a slither of consciousness that reminded her that, "I'm a lady!" I guess the point I want to make here is that your virtuousness should not only reflect your behavior, but who you are as a woman. I don't mean to come off as some guru *(which I am not)*, but the idea of virtuousness shouldn't be new to you. It is already a part of **You must <u>willfully</u> accept virtuousness as a central attribute of your God-given genetic code. The enemy to this in your life is compromise.** your feminine psyche; you simple need to embrace it.

In your *subconscious* mind, the creator has endowed you with an appetite for splendor and moral excellence. To put it simply: *"Your father has already given you a mind to accept nothing less than the best!"* That's not being conceited, but comfortable in your own mind with what you were always wired to think, demand and accept for yourself. Now, I don't mean to be brash, but "woman" you better get with the program! I think it's quite clear these days that some of you have simply lost your "God-given" minds! Therefore, as it appears, *compromise* has become the basis upon which some decide to govern all their life decisions.

Madam President

In this day, there is the belief that as a nation we are on the cusp of seeing something as unprecedented as our first female commander-in-chief. I say why wait for Hillary? Take control of your own life, evaluate where you are at this moment. Are you where you want to be? Are you doing what you want to do as a career? How is the quality of your relationships? What kind of woman do you want to be? What sort of decisions are you allowing to govern your life? I think it's safe to say, "Madam President," that you are the commander-in-chief concerning your own life. Take responsibility for where you want to go and *how* you plan to get there.

The quality you accept and the manner in which you elect to represent yourself or lifestyle is yours to decide. My only suggestion is that you rid your life of all weapons of "self" destruction, especially compromise, self-hatred, and phoniness. Become the woman you were born to be. I'm not encouraging you to merely win the game, but to change it! The way you do this is by ultimately changing how it gets played. Are you willing to evolve the way you think as a woman? I don't want you to think like me, but rather be a woman phenomenally. Realize that's what I am after here, you embracing the phenomenon that you were uniquely and beautifully made by God.

The New Normal

At this stage in our dialogue, I hope that the flower of virtuousness is being watered in the recesses of your spirit. I want you to allow this consciousness to ignite within you the flame of hope that your quality of life can get better.

You have inside you the power to change whatever is intolerable to you by simply raising the standard of what you are willing to accept.

Pick a different color as your favorite! Don't you think it's time to establish a "new normal" in your life? Up to this point, maybe you've become too predictable. Compromise will do that to you if the rudder of your life isn't set in a clear direction. At this moment, I want to challenge you to set a new path for yourself and for your own life. Start by opening your mind to change. Do you remember the following statement from earlier?

"A woman's virtuousness is the undercurrent in her life which should temper every facet. Self-image, self-worth, self-government, moral character, love, relationships, family, business, everything that encompasses her life should be marked by it."

Moving forward, I will endeavor to discuss each of those areas in your life that can be affected and reformed by the God-given power of virtuousness within you. So, come, let us go deeper.

The Super Model

The premise of this book is based upon the admiration I have for a particular woman. She inspires me to become a better man. She is my muse, and so I like to refer to her as "the super model" because her life clearly lays out the inherent traits of virtuousness. These qualities are spread widely across the spectrum of her lifestyle. She is a woman of many colors and, frankly, there is much to learn from her example. From this moment on, we will be examining the book of Proverbs as we take a very systematic look at the tapestry of her life.

*"Who can find a virtuous woman? For her worth is far more valuable than rubies. The heart of her husband is so secure that he has no need for any other treasure." - **Proverbs 31:10, 11***

For the moment, please ignore the fact that she's a wife and instead focus on her as an individual. The first thing I want you to take away from this account is that without question "she is an asset." It's not simply about her looks or her body. Her greatest strength is in "who she is," and everything that strength encompasses. Do you know that the quality of who you are is what really makes you invaluable? Don't place the greatest stock in your looks or body, because usually that only serves as a means to cheapen you.

The Character Factor

I know that "moral character" is not the most common theme in today's culture. That's not what sells, but it is vitally essential to your identity and even quality of life. Sure, there are the few, yet growing number of women, out there who put their stock in the wrong things. They tend to unconsciously begin to cheapen themselves through compromise and are often easily deterred and distracted. Some women even begin to lose valuable momentum while in pursuit of their dreams or ambitions, simply because of their lack of character.

Character is perhaps the most significant factor that determines what you really bring into any situation. Intellectual or moral integrity is simply one's soundness of mind to make the right decisions. Surely, we all need that!

Compromised and driven by vain pursuits, they usually abandon the "standard" of their own virtuousness. In fact, there are those who even avail themselves as mere pawns to the TV, music, and entertainment industries. Let's keep it real! The porn industry alone profits millions, (for the most part) on the *willful*, and *consenting* sexual exploitation of women. When it comes to the moral or intellectual fabric of who you are as a person, what do you stand for? Is your standard uncompromising or do you *willingly* consent to your own exploitation? Judge yourself, weigh the value of your own decisions.

"She has sought wool and linen, and she works at whatever is the delight of her hands. She has proved to be like the ships of a merchant. From far away she brings in her food." - Proverbs 31:13, 14

Notice that the account revealed that she sought enjoyment in what she was good at. Her comparison to a "merchant ship" spoke directly to the depths of her substance and productivity. Consider this statement: *"From far away she brings in her food."* This simply means that there were no limits to her determination for success.

"She has considered a field and proceeded to obtain it; from the works of her hands she has planted a vineyard. She has girded her hips with strength, and she invigorates her arms. She has sensed that her trading is good."
- Proverbs 31:16, 18

Find contentment in what you are good at. It doesn't matter what you are doing right now as a career, don't be afraid to seek the skills or education you need to accomplish your goals.

Immediately, I want you to notice she was so "totally invested" in her own achievement that there simply wasn't time to be distracted. Obviously, this woman worked very hard to make everything that was "hers" a success. I also love the fact that she is self-aware and considers "all" she has to offer, to be good. Now that's the key, harnessing every gift you possess. Identify every ounce of your potential and then do something with it!

Jealousy Is for The Lazy

Coveting someone else's things or success is such a waste of your time, since you have the *capabilities* to get the same for yourself. Jealousy is for the lazy! Those who are constantly driven by covetousness tend to be people who are too lazy or *un-invested* in what they have themselves, so they're always discontented. There's nothing wrong with learning from another's success, just be willing to "work" towards your own. This invested approach will work in life, relationships, marriage, business, and anything else that you do. Take the time to develop yourself or to at least identify what you uniquely possess that is of worth. Don't be the sort who obsesses over what someone else has, but make the conscious decision to steward what *you* have.

"She makes tapestry for herself; her clothing is fine linen and purple. Strength and honor are her clothing" - *Proverbs 31:22, 25*

Nowadays it is not a secret that when it comes to fashion, women enjoy the lion's share. What you wear tends to say a lot about you, especially how you feel about yourself. Above, we see that she adorned herself with nice things. I really love to see a woman accessorize, who's trendy and classy. So, I can totally appreciate this woman's sense of self-respect. In her case, perhaps the clothes directly reflected the woman.

What Are Your Clothes Saying About You?

Certainly, I am not the one to judge anybody's fashion sense, since I admittedly have little. Still, there is a point worth making here. What you wear does say something about you?

If you were totally naked, that would be saying something. Don't you think so? Thus, how you adorn yourself should say as much about you, as it does your sense of fashion.

Have you ever gone out or been at a nightspot and seen a young lady dressed in a scandalous way? Yet when she is approached or addressed in an assuming manner, she responds with: *"Just because I'm dressed this way doesn't make me a whore!"*

Now to be fair, I will say that she is correct, but you have to at least admit that it is awfully confusing. Respectfully, she is not a streetwalker, but perhaps she *is* wearing the uniform! All right, up to this point we have been able to take a good look into the feminine and intellectual psyche of an incredible woman.

My hope is that you have truly been able to take away something valuable for yourself. Strategically, I now want to shift the focus back to *you* in the next conversation as we take a closer look at how uniquely gifted and *phenomenal* you are. There is simply more to you than you know.

The Standard Of Virtuousness

How did you feel about this conversation?

_____
_____
_____

*What are some personal things you took from this conversation?

_____
_____
_____

*Do you have any personal experiences you are comfortable talking about?

_____
_____
_____

*Name 10 Queens you are going to share this conversation with.

1._____ 6._____
2._____ 7._____
3._____ 8._____
4._____ 9._____
5._____ 10._____

By the way, here are some talking points...

What Is Virtuousness?

-*The uncompromising standard.*
-*That "wonderful" feeling.*
-*Virtuousness is a part of your "God-given" genetic code.*

The Super Model

-*You are an asset*
-*The character factor*
-*Don't be a victim.*
-*Move from "commoner," to queen.*

Jealousy Is for The Lazy

-*Find contentment in what "you" are good at.*
-*Get "totally invested" in your own personal development and success.*
-*Steward what "you" have to offer someone else.*

What Are Your Clothes Saying About You?

-*Be fashionable, but "represent yourself" virtuously.*
-*What uniform are you wearing?*

5

THE PLANTING OF DESTINY

Up front, I must say that you have made a deliberate decision to put your face in these pages. Because of that, you've set yourself on a collision course with something truly powerful beyond measure. It's going to transform you! It will stir up the very creative juices within you. That *something* is the revelation of who *you* are! Can you handle that? Now, we are going to talk about the planting of destiny. I know this may seem a bit strange, but before we get moving, there's a simple request I have of you? Repeat this for me, but in your James Brown voice! Say," ***The planting of destiny!"***

All right, now let me ask, have any of you ever planted anything before? Sure, you have! Now tell me, what was the first thing that you needed? A seed! I find it amusing to be discussing this particular subject with you. Specifically, as a woman, you can appreciate the power and potential of a planted seed. Actually, you are carrying one right now! So much *value* and *creativity* have been deliberately invested in the soil of your life. You just need to simply let it out!

The Steward and The Tree

What's your favorite food? Pasta, chicken, banana pudding, shrimp, French fries, or Philly Cheese steak? Great! In other words, if I were to break each of those dishes down to their least common denominator, I would be left with nothing more than seeds. What I want to bring into clear view is the extreme significance of a seed. Every seed has a mandated purpose, to bring forth its designated fruit. Do you believe that? Orange seeds should beget oranges. Pineapple seeds should beget pineapples, so on and so forth. Let me tell you a story.

"A man had a fig tree growing in his vineyard, and he went to look for fruit on it, but did not find any. So he said to the man who took care of the vineyard, for three years now I've been coming to look for fruit on this fig tree and haven't found any. Cut it down! Why should it use up the soil? But he answered and said to him, Sir, let it alone this year also until I dig around it and fertilize it." –Luke 13:6-8

I think it was a bit over the top for the owner of the vineyard to simply want to cut down the tree. Although I can understand his frustration, I mean it was a tree; shouldn't there have been some fruit to bear? Did you notice what the steward of the vineyard said: **"let it alone this year also until I dig around it and fertilize it?"** Why had he not done something sooner? Was the tree really to blame after all or was it just the work of an unfaithful steward?

You Are Carrying a Seed

Consider your life. Ever wonder whether there is something more to you? Well, there is! Something's "inside" you, it's a seed. In fact, you were born with it, but don't just take my word for it! Watch this! In the beginning, God said, "Let the land *produce* vegetation: seed-bearing plants and trees on the land that bear fruit with seed in it, according to their various kinds. He saw that it was good." You see, that was the natural order, everything had been designed with the ability to *carry* and *produce* a seed. Every beast of the field, fowl of the air, every creeping thing, *including you,* carries within itself, a "seed."

At this moment, we are going to do a very short exercise. I want you to think about the word *produce*. Take a few moments... Ok, whatever's in your head keep it there? Next, I want you to think of a cow. "Wait for it... wait for it..." Now honestly, what came to mind? I will assume that right away you were thinking steak, cheese, milk, leather, etc. Since what I had hoped to capture in your mind is the word *product*! Why? Because in essence, you can't just think of a cow without being confronted by the vastness of its gross domestic product. A cow is responsible for more than reproducing or merely carrying a seed; its life is undoubtedly more significant. I'll prove it to you!

The Cow and Its Gross Product

Can you say Nike, Reebok, Addidas, Puma, McDonalds, Burger King, NBA, and NFL? Those are s just to name a few. Each of those all together make up only a *portion* of the companies and products, which reflects "a cow's" gross domestic product. Well friend, does your life carry more purpose and significance than a cow? It most certainly does! Forget about where you are right now. Stop talking about what you don't have. Change the atmosphere of your thought life today. I can still remember when my son's mother first discovered she was expecting. We were married at the time and so once the pregnancy became official, we began paying closer attention to what was going on inside of her.

She was carrying something, and it mattered. It would ultimately bring about changes in every part of her lifestyle. Everything began to systematically change. Her appetite, attitude, mindset, and appearance (beautifully I must say) all evolved to meet the growing demand of her pregnancy. Have you ever stopped to consider the fact that *you* too are *carrying* something? It's important that in your life you begin paying closer attention to what you're carrying. There is something, and it's alive in you right now, kicking, and screaming for your attention! It's something that demands changes in your lifestyle as it wills to drive all your motivations.

You Are Pregnant!

Ms., just in case you haven't noticed, I am here to tell you something extraordinary. Despite the hang-ups, excuses or any perceived obstacles in your life right now, you're pregnant! Futility has become a thing of the past. Dear woman, not only will you produce, but you're going to bring into being the mandated *purpose* for your existence. In fact, as a matter of agreement, wherever you are at this second, I want you to confess this to yourself out loud. Say this! ***"There is a seed of destiny within me!"*** Say: ***"I will bring into being the mandated purpose for my existence!"*** It's so necessary for you to hear yourself declaring those truths. Why, you ask?

Well, because you are stirring up the gift or (seed) that is fluttering on the inside of you. And as we move forward, line by line, embrace the fact that you are actively carrying a seed. This is the dawn of a new day. Change must become real in every aspect of your life, as the time has come for your habits and tendencies to evolve as you now make the necessary adjustments in your life. Begin to identify what gifts, ideas, and God-given ambitions are teaming within you. I pray even now that your spiritual, emotional, and intellectual appetites will change for the better. Remember, "you are pregnant," and so you must start feeding the health, creativity and growth you want to see birthed in your life.

Believe in What You Are Carrying

I am the proud father of an eight-year-old son named Caleb. He's a bit of a budding artist who loves to draw different things. I can still remember an instance where he had drawn a depiction of a dog and one of me. He ran to me and said, *"Daddy look, I drew a picture for you! Do you like it?"* Let me just say that what I saw looked more like a moon-rock than a dog, and I was a stick figure with a head the size of Mars. Yet, without even blinking an eye, I said to him, *"Wow! Thanks, big guy, I think your picture is awesome!"* Frankly, it's goes without saying that I have *total* faith in Caleb's hopes and abilities. There isn't a soul on earth who could ever make me feel differently. So, with that in mind, there's a modern-day philosopher whom I would like to quote:

"I believe I can fly! I believe I can touch the sky! I think about it every night and day. I believe I can soar! I see myself running through an open door! I believe I can fly!" -R. Kelly

Hopefully, those sentiments resonate within your life as well. Since, above all, *you* alone must have faith in what you're carrying on the inside. No one else must believe, nor should they care more about your life than you do. There are many things about you that are truly wonderful. Woman, the simple fact is that you have a definite contribution to make, and it is valuable!

Steward What Has Been Invested in You

Can you get something out of nothing? Can you take a cookie from an empty cookie jar? The answer to both is *no,* unless there is an official deposit. It would be an utter shame for me to inspire you in every known way, but neglect to address the fact that God has a great deal invested in you. Consider the Rockefellers, Bill Gates, or Donald Trump. Most people today can admit that they're successful, perhaps even the shrewdest of investors. In any case, I tend to suspect that even *they* expect a return on their investments. Well, why would God be any different? After all, it is *He* who has "given" gifts to all humanity.

My sole objective here is to remind you that in His eyes, your life is a valuable investment. Therefore, as you examine yourself in this season, know that your personal stewardship is vitally important. That's going to be the key to any significant breakthroughs for you. As I pointed out earlier, realize that there are some very strategic things happening in and around you. Even this very moment you reading this book is not a mere coincidence. In fact, before you were ever conceived, God had already foreseen this actual second of your life. And you know what? He wants your undivided attention.

The Crossroad

Ultimately, there have been others in your bloodline before you, who were called to greatness. Those in whom were placed great gifting and destiny, yet due to either ignorance, doubt, or sheer disregard, they caused themselves to *default* on the investment, which was made "in" them. Do you find any of what I've said to be spooky or strange? Look around you? What's in your family? Is there a history of achievement and success? How are the relational bonds? Are they healthy or dysfunctional? Certainly, I can't answer any of those questions for you, but what I *do* sense is that you are at a crossroads. This is *your* defining moment, so go ahead and seize it!

Go ahead, I dare you to let go of every limitation that will keep you from charting a healthier path. Am I saying you are better than anyone else? No, you are just different, and that is why God's gaze has fallen on you. Frankly speaking, your life is supposed to be representative of something different, fresh, and new, that God is doing in your bloodline. Everything about you is contrary to anything that's ever been done in your family. Even now, there are certain things warring for controlling authority and influence over your lifestyle. There are certain mindsets, attitudes, or "belief systems and generational "obstructions" that have traditionally stood in the way of others before you, and I am willing to suggest that they are actively challenging your life right now.

A Bird of a Different Feather

Whether it is prevalent sickness, disease, lack, poverty, dysfunctional behavior, etc. you must realize who you are and rise up! Believe it or not, you were born to prevail against the contrary winds of doubt, fear, and indecision of the past. You are a bird of a totally different feather! What others have struggled with and winked at in the past you aren't wired to accept as the norm. The *shift* starts with you!

Therefore, in the coming days and months of your pregnancy, get ready for some pressure and confrontation. Personally, you are going to have to openly embrace the growing disassociation between yourself and generational discrepancies of the past that exist in your bloodline. Understand also, during this time of growth and deliberate changes in your life, that you will be perhaps accused, berated, and misunderstood. However, if you will just push through the pain of those contractions, I promise you that in the end, you will deliver! As I bring closure to this conversation, keep these words in mind:

"Before you were born, God ordained your life as profitable to Him as well as the nations. Your life matters and it has a sure purpose." –Derrick J. Little

The Planting Of Destiny

How did you feel about this conversation?

_____
_____
_____
_____

*What are some personal things you took from this conversation?

_____
_____
_____

*Do you have any personal experiences you are comfortable talking about?

_____
_____
_____

*Name 10 Queens are you going to share this conversation with?

1._____ 6._____
2._____ 7._____
3._____ 8._____
4._____ 9._____
5._____ 10._____

By the way, here are some talking points...

The Planting!

-The steward and the tree.

-You are carrying a seed.

-The cow and her gross product.

-You are pregnant!

-Believe in what you are carrying.

The Crossroad!

-A bird of a different feather.

-The shift starts with you.

-Steward what has been "invested" in you.

-This is "your" moment.

-Generational obstructions.

-You must rise up!

6

BECOME A VISIONARY

What are you doing with your life? Are you content with your present state of being? Today is the day for you to cast aside every distraction that stifles your productivity. At this moment, I am going to assume that you are someone who's extremely gifted and creative. Some company probably employs you and you're very good at what you do. How much wealth do you think your productivity, giftedness and creativity has profited others more than they have you? My point here is that your life has a purpose, and part of that is to be fruitful, multiply, and have dominion. Allow me to bring something else to your attention. There is a certain passage of scripture in Genesis which states: *"And God blessed them, and God said to them, be fruitful, and multiply, and replenish the earth, and subdue it: and have dominion."* -Gen. 1:28

Right there, I want you to particularly notice the word ***"them,"*** it is referring to both men and women. Do you know that you were born to be dominating, to conquer, and not to be conquered? Traditionally, men are pegged as visionaries. It is potentially our most definitive trait; however, I want you to know that even, as a woman, you should be a visionary as well!

Shouldn't A Queen Be a Visionary?

Isn't a king supposed to be forward-looking? Well, what about a queen, shouldn't she be a visionary too? I believe that if more women will simply take notice of themselves and their own life that there wouldn't be such a misplaced sense of competition. There's no question about it, God made women competitive. Thus, many just need to channel that "spirit of conquest" towards their own life's purpose and vision. The point I am making here is that you must have a vision for your life just as a man is expected to have one for himself. That is why this book isn't geared to help you question a man, but to challenge you to cultivate the power within you.

I want to encourage you to become a visionary. From this perspective, understand that there was never supposed to be any difference between men and women. God gave gifts to men and women alike. He said to *"them"* be fruitful, multiply, and have dominion. It is also written: ***"Your gifts will make room for you and set you before great men."*** Know this. There are gifts, dreams, and ambitions that were *planted* in you; and those very same things, *if cultivated*, will cause your life to become fruitful! They will carve out a place of fulfillment and success for you. Frankly, I submit to you that it's not your body or looks which should elevate or sustain you, but ultimately what you do with what's on the inside. You're not an object, but a person first.

Make This a Personal Matter

Right now, I want you to personalize the fact that you must cultivate your gifts and do something with your life. So it doesn't really matter whether you are married or single, you should still have a vision. Why? Well, because it serves as a compass for where you want to go and practically a vision helps to bring greater definition to the character of your life. When a man or woman has a vision, it should serve as a buffer to the tenor of their decisions. If you have a clear understanding of what you want to achieve, that should have some effect on everything you say, think and do.

Now am I saying that you should act or even think like a man?   Certainly not, be a woman, phenomenally! But it's time to really start articulating your own life's vision.

"Write the vision; make it plain on tablets, so he may run who reads it. For still the vision awaits its appointed time; it hastens to the end—it will not lie. If it seems slow, wait for it; it will surely come; it will not delay." - Habakkuk 2:2, 3

What do you want out of life? Where do you see yourself going in your career? What are you doing with those ideas and witty inventions? Are you interested in becoming an entrepreneur? Do you want to be a homeowner? Do you want to get married some day and start a family? Plan for what you want and then work your plan.

Do Not Make Excuses

"Excuses are monuments of nothingness. They build bridges to nowhere, those of us who use these tools of incompetence, seldom become anything, but nothing at all." – Someone Successful

This is just something else to think about as you get started because I feel some people just allow anything to become an easy excuse. Don't let anything deter you any longer! Even being a wife or mother shouldn't be an excuse for not following a dream or executing your life's vision. Let there be no limitation to your greatness! Only you can determine where your stopping point will be. Go ahead and open a business, dust off that great idea, pull those manuscripts back out! Don't you dare be afraid to execute a plan for your life! If you're single, run with it! If you're married, run with it! If you're a mother, run with it!

Having a vision doesn't guarantee that life won't sometimes get in the way, but you just need to remain focused and diligent. Understand that in life, every journey will present challenges, but excuses will never get you anywhere. Make the conscious decision not to limit your own potential by making excuses for why you can't accomplish something. In an earlier conversation, I suggested that perhaps some women should practice ***abstinence*** as a means of refocusing themselves. ***Come on now, don't let that scare you, just keep reading.***

Your Vision Must Be Bigger Than You!

To this point, sometimes men and women alike allow promiscuity and the "revolving doors" of relationships to become detractors.

Such things can easily ensnare you when there isn't a vision to keep you focused and motivated in the meantime. You must possess a belief in something bigger than yourself if you're going to achieve anything significant. Sex is not bigger than you! Dating relationships are not bigger than you! Both are necessary and have their own time and place. Therefore, each should be put into proper perspective. Abstinence can perhaps help to stem the tide of premature pregnancies, disease, and any other issues which often impede the progress and quality of life for many women. Take hold of your life by taking control of yourself!

Get Out of Your Own Way

Have you ever heard someone use the phrase: *"Check yourself before you wreck yourself?"* Well, at this moment in your life if you want your experiences to be meaningful and enriching, then certain things must change. Make time for the kinds of things you want to achieve. If further education or technical training is what you need to do to follow through on your vision, then do what is necessary to attain it.

Remember, Jealousy Is for The Lazy

Stay focused on your personal goals. Don't allow the vision killers of doubt, insecurity, laziness and procrastination to rob your life of great achievement. Do you remember the *"super model"* we observed in the book of Proverbs? She was always driven by discipline and completely *invested* in her own vision. Take her example and use it for your own life as you lay out a strategy for success in your own life. Also, keep in mind something I shared in an earlier conversation:

"Coveting someone else's things or success is such a waste of your time since you have the capabilities to get the same for yourself. Jealousy is for the lazy. Those who find themselves constantly driven by covetousness tend to be people who are too lazy or un-invested in what they have themselves, so they're always discontented. There's truly nothing wrong with learning from another's success, just be willing to work towards your own.

This kind of invested approach will work in every area of life, relationships, marriage, business, and anything else you do. Take the time to develop yourself or to at least identify what you uniquely possess that is of worth. Don't be the sort who obsesses over what someone else has to offer you, but determine to steward what you have."

Stay on The Mountain

Finally, I want to slow the pace a little as we dive into what I believe to be another major distraction. Settling! There seems to be a moral and intellectual crisis among many women today as they find themselves *lowering* their standards of their virtuousness. Consider this. Do you think that if, *for some reason*, every woman in the world were to be placed at the top of Mount Everest, that some man wouldn't attempt to scale its heights to reach them? Of course, they

Don't think like that, I say you need to settle yourself at the top of the mountain and may "the best man" come on up!

would! The problem with some women today is that they are afraid that if they set their standards too high, men won't meet them.

Be patient as you embrace the *standard* of your virtuousness! Don't *depreciate* yourself by simply lowering your standards.

Remember, queen, you just need to set yourself up in a "high place" and stay there! Settle yourself, when you are truly focused on established goals and strategies you won't be easily distracted by trivial things. There will be time for relationships, so don't rush into anything. When I say keep your standards high, what I am really saying is, stay focused on where you want to go in your life. When you meet that special person, let it happen naturally.

The Big Compromise

Very quickly, I want to bring back into focus something we touched on in an earlier conversation. What is virtuousness? It is the uncompromising standard of thinking that reflects your moral and intellectual state of being.

When you decide to lower your standards, you lose focus on what you want and it opens the door to the *undermining* notion of *compromise*, which affects the way you govern your behavior. Suddenly, you may

"A woman's virtuousness is the undercurrent in her life, which should temper every facet. Self-image, self-worth, self-government, moral character, love, relationships, family, business, everything that encompasses her life should be marked by it."

find yourself off the path you have set for your life, which isn't good, because your time and talents are valuable. You don't have a moment to waste by getting sucked into a "man hunt." When you allow that to happen, a shift occurs and the odds are, you're the one who's searching! You're the one who's calling! You're the one who's giving everything away just so you can find yourself a life-sucking parasite who calls himself a man. He drives *your* car! You give *him* money, and *buy* his clothes! If that is the way you *willfully* decide to compromise yourself, then the following suggestions are specifically for you.

Don't Aide the Immaturity of Men

"Don't complain about how men don't respect you! Stop crying over the fact that most of the men you meet seem to be more interested in sex than they are in you! And stop saying, there aren't any good men."

Understand that when you compromise the standard of your virtuousness, what you are doing is helping to hinder the needed maturity of men. I know this notion seems to be somewhat ridiculous, but please realize that some men either have very little or no desire to mature as a consequence of this behavior. A man should have a vision for himself, which means he should be driven by his own meaningful life pursuits. If sex is all that inspires him, then he is a man who isn't ready to mature. Sex is a basic need we all have, but there is a time and place for it.

Also, understand that if you want respect, you must first decide to respect yourself. It is truly time for some women to stop governing themselves in these compromising types of ways if they expect to be loved, appreciated, and treated as they should be treated. Do not *expect* from a man what you do not *demand* from yourself. I say that mainly because if you have low standards you will make yourself prone to *accepting* things that are totally unacceptable. Ultimately, you must ask *yourself* this question. Will I allow a man to get a license to own a dog, yet it not be required for him to make that type of commitment to me?

You Have the Greatest Value!

Can a man get everything he wants from you without a license? Seriously, I want you to ponder that. Are you saying that he's got to have a *license* to drive a car or to do mostly anything else, but he can actually come untrained, unskilled, and just have his way with you?

Certainly, this sort of foolishness must cease. You're too *valuable* for such disrespectful, depreciating, immature behavior to be tolerated any longer. However, I want to be very careful in stating that obviously not all men fall into this category.

Surely, there are responsible, hardworking, thoughtful, driven men out here in the world. I feel it would be totally irresponsible to overlook the fact that not every woman is a victim. Rather, there are some women who exploit themselves due to their own vices. So, at this moment, I want to say that you have the greatest influence over your own life, as well as what happens in it. Therefore, I will leave you with one final suggestion: Get out of your own way.

7

THE RIFT

A growing problem exists among many women today; they're not connecting well with one another anymore. This disconnect has created a rift which is affecting how they relate, interact, and learn from one another. As we engage in this final conversation, I would like to start by asking a few questions. Do you feel women are competitive? What do you think of women's interaction with one another these days? Do you see more interactions that are positive or negative? Can this rift be simply based upon whether another woman wants what you have? Is it a man, wanting more money or a better career?

Is the basis of *competition* really, looks, sex, and social status? Do you feel that this sort of behavior is more prevalent today than perhaps in any other generation? Unfortunately, these types of questions need to be seriously considered and then brought into proper perspective. Unlike in previous conversations, I want you to start by personally considering what seven other women had to say concerning the matter at hand before I attempt to offer any perspective on the issue.

What Other Women Are Saying?

Tracy Says: "I am a petite, intelligent redhead. At school, I dressed like a hobo and pretty much ignored men just so I was not considered a threat to my female friends. As a result, I had some good female friends. These days, I refuse to sell myself short anymore and it has cost me most of my old friendships, as well as potential new friends. I have an awful time with other women – even my oldest female friends hide their husbands and boyfriends away from me. I have never stolen or even flirted with anyone's boyfriend/husband, but men do give me too much attention for most women's comfort.

It doesn't matter how I react to the attention or even if I make a point of rebuffing it – the women will whip their men away and if I am not cut off completely, we will forever continue to meet up as just "the girls." It makes no difference whether I have a boyfriend or not. It has come to the point where I am ready to give up trying to have proper friendships with women – they are just too irrational in their competitiveness and insecurities. For me, in most cases, it is nearly impossible to pacify those feelings enough to have a friendship."

Linda Says: "My boyfriend's boss who used him as a sounding board for all of her woes has been very cruel, not only to me but to him as well. This is an older, married woman who resents me because she feels I have taken her "friend" away. She is married, but her husband has tuned her out. I am also younger and take care of myself. Another negative view I have is this, I would hope to inspire other women, but it seems it is easier to simply be mean. Bottom line is that I have had to smile and take it, from her and from the other women she keeps in her office.

At times, I feel attacked. I never told my boyfriend to discontinue his friendship with her. I understood it. He is a friend with her husband, who also works there. Unfortunately, she has destroyed their friendship. There are times when I am upset over it all and it does affect my relationship since it is the only issue we argue about. Of course, this woman would be happy to see us break up. I have no one to talk to, so I'm sure it's annoying for him to hear. Grrrrrrrr! Unnecessary behavior on her part, and it is only getting worse."

[1]*Cassandra George Sturges, Psy.D Says*: "From the time that little girls are born, society expects them to fit into a certain mold, a particular role and possess certain characteristics. The characteristics that are expected of them are assumed to be natural and inflexible. Little girls are always instructed on how they

---

[1] Quoted from http://www.triond.com

should look, how they should behave and how they should feel. Little girls should be beautiful, dainty, neat, polite, nurturing and well behaved. When she deviates from the identity given to her by society she becomes disillusioned about her self-worth and role in society. This is the root of self-hatred and low self-esteem for many women.

Women compete with each other at a societal level. The criteria for winning is usually set by others and the results are subjective and intangible. Women are usually judged by characteristics they have little control over; something that they did not create, and which exists outside of themselves, such as their physical appearance. Her success is based on subjective, biased, external validation by others. She can't see how to beat her rival because her rival is in no more control over the outcome than she is. How can you really be more beautiful than another woman when the decision is nothing more than someone else's opinion of beauty?

How can you change someone's personal preference for a certain body size and shape, a particular eye color or a fondness for blondes? How many people are needed to think that you are beautiful before it is a valid or meaningful judgment? Who do you need to tell you that you are beautiful before you can believe it to be true…construction workers, truck drivers, the man walking down the street, your pastor, the Pope, your boss? Women compete with each other for male attention and compliments as if it feeds their self-worth and self-esteem.

Women try to dress sexier and have shapelier bodies than other women. Women are so busy competing with each other for male attention that they do not have the psychological, intellectual, or emotional insight to change the social climate that is causing them to suffer from low self-esteem."

Stacy Says: "Over the years, I have come to seriously hate some women. I have been hounded out of many a job through jealous, insecure, nasty women. And not just young women either, older ones are just as bad too! I've had to tolerate catty comments, silent treatment, stitched up for mistakes that I've never made. I used to be confident with a witty personality, but the years of people chipping away at it have made me a shadow of my former self. I can no longer go out for a night out with my boyfriend, as the women in his group of friends are viciously bitchy towards me.

I've come home from a night-out in floods of tears, as I have had to endure snide comments, yawning in my face, and all because I'm confident in my own skin and like stylish clothing. These girls have got issues with their weight, and therefore take it out on me and hate it if any of the attention is taken away from them. I consider myself a down to earth, laid back person who likes to get along with everyone, but women just don't like me. If you are the type of woman who is constantly self-deprecating, and constantly putting yourself down and dressing like a piece of shit then other women will take to you."

Evelyn Says: "I am a pretty woman who works in an all-female office of fuglies - inside and out. When I got Lasik surgery done about two years ago, it really went downhill with their

94

behaviors. They are all married, I am divorced, and dating. Other divorced women exclude me from events because they view me as competition. I also look very young for my age. The only women who are decent with me are other pretty women, as well as older women who are no longer competitive. I'm not stuck up or a bitch, really it just seems like there is a "pretty prejudice"! I have been at the receiving end of some really horrific behavior."

Lindsey Says: "Women today appear to be nastier and more bitter towards each other than ever. The difference is that now, it's all out in the open.

Before anyone bashes feminism, it did encourage some sisterhood between women. I'm 31, and I can remember a time when women stuck together more than they do now; it wasn't that long ago. Women don't need to compete for men as much as they think they do because men are less fussy than women. I know this to be the case because I am a lesbian (yes!) who wears short hair and no makeup and I've still met men who were interested in me. That means the average feminine woman is not going to have much difficulty getting a man. In fact, all the bitching to other women puts men off them as they all have female friends, sisters and mothers. Also, women are now competing for resources much more than they had to in the past. In the past, the only way to get resources was through a man, so most people married for life. Today, women are getting a taste of what the wider world is like and how cut-throat it is. I think this is a good thing. because when feminism was at its height, most women were at the same level, low-paid, etc., men were the competitors. But today, other women

95

are competitors too, so sister-ship went and women went back to the default. I believe that for most straight women, the mere sight

of an attractive woman causes her adrenal glands to kick up her flight or fight response. Just because you're a woman and she is a woman does not mean she is on your side.

There will never be a sisterhood of women that can work. Just like there has never been worldwide unity between men. It's a sad shame."

Daniela Says: "I'm 45 and I've been badly treated by women from the time I was a little girl. The pattern started with my older sisters, who resented the fact that I was cuter than they were. Sadly, it continued throughout school, as some girls were horrid to me. I am a nice person, and I have had it up to here with other women. I've given up trying to be friends with them, they are dysfunctional, vile bitches, two-faced, begrudging, neurotically insecure, and the rest. In my mind, men are far easier to get along with. I'm a female saying this, but I really think women are evil, not all, but too many. They can't resist a cutting remark any chance they get, but always too cowardly to say anything outright to your face.

The backbiting just makes me hate them more. I've been repeatedly ostracized by other women just for being perceived as a tomboy. Ostracizing someone for no good reason is cruel. Women do this all the time, and it's always for some petty, stupid reason, or no reason at all. I've learned to accept the fact that I won't have any female friends. I think it's a shame, because if these women would bother to get to know me, they'd find that I'm not all that different from them and that I am a nice person – but they haven't bothered. They just want to hate."

May I Offer Another Perspective?

If I may, my take is that perhaps the increased aggression or competitiveness among women today is relative to their growing emergence in the work place. I read an article on the Internet the other day, which claimed that women account for more than 53% of the new businesses being created currently. Wow, now that's just amazing! You could say that nowadays women are finally "getting in the game," while in times past they were held on the side-lines. What I simply mean by "on the side-lines" is that for many decades, the potential of women was generally limited to their domestic significance.

As a matter of proper perspective, I deliberately denoted a woman's domestic contribution as something truly significant! Why? Well, because it is too easy to ignore amidst this type of conversation. I watched my mom do the job up close. Once my dad left, she raised eight of us alone. I came to realize that being a mother is a tremendous responsibility! If there were no mothers, we wouldn't have *competitiveness* in society, we simply wouldn't exist! I just need to make this point clear, I don't believe a woman's position in the work place subsequently renders the role she plays as a mom and teacher any less important.

Women Hold Tremendous Significance

Hypothetically speaking, if one were to take away the significance of these roles women play and simply shift all of the focus to their social status and corporate ladder climbing, what type of society would we have? Certainly, parenting isn't just exclusively a woman's responsibility, but the part they play can never be duplicated or overstated, period. Yet, today if all of a sudden, a woman's domestic significance is no longer honorable or *acceptable,* then where does that leave our children, families, and society?

If you were to take away the invaluable contribution women bring to the stabilization of our society, then that would be catastrophic. Furthermore, by no means do I fault women for promoting the notion that there is more to them than their domestic significance. I agree, but not to the point where I would encourage any woman to hate who she is as a mother or to overlook who she is as a teacher or as a wife.

The fact is that, as individuals, women do possess greater capabilities beyond their domestic significance. However, this particular point was worth making because it is *often* a topic that tends to gets lost in the progressive shuffle of today. Essentially, the most epic casualty women suffer today is due to strained *social* interactions, which cripples their social development as well as their *relationships.*

A Casualty of War

Apparently, many women don't get along and that's no secret, but the fact remains that they need each other. This ongoing rift is one of the main causes of a widening gap between women along relational, social, and generational lines, which are all vital to them. How so? Well, practically this type of dysfunctional behavior greatly undermines the dynamic societal elements of support, teaching, and mentorship that have traditionally served as major sources of empowerment to women for generations.

The careful transfer of wisdom and guidance had always taken shape within the tender confines of relationships. For women, in theory, wisdom and guidance was generally conveyed to one another across social or generational lines. There was once an acceptance, an open understanding to the extreme significance given to such relationships. Whether it was to be a mother, daughter, granny, auntie, cousin or friend women needed to have healthy social interaction with one another. These relational bonds are still what should be rendering the love, guidance, and a wealth of life experiences that women need. Why? Because they help to carve out a path of development and substance for generations of women to follow. Undoubtedly, the significance of this element is still necessary, irreplaceable and undeniable.

Do Women Really Grasp Their Impact?

The problem nowadays is that many of the interpersonal bonds women need are strained. They aren't really relating or communicating well with each other. What a sad commentary because the fact is that women are too valuable to be entangled by such dysfunction. Personally, I think there is a certain sway that women hold over the moral conscience in our society. I firmly believe that when the qualities of women's lives are hindered socially, relationally, and economically, society as a whole is greatly affected. Generally, I feel that some women today don't see themselves as being that significant. Here's my point, if one were to completely remove the contributions of women from society, humanity would be lost. Sure, maybe that sounds a bit dramatic, but it's true.

The same can be said for men, although there never seems to be a shortage of people or ideology that often touts a man's impact. The point I'm stressing here is the extreme *value* of women. Frankly, men can no longer refute that, but rather the question remains, how many women *themselves* still fail to grasp it? I am certain that if more women truly understood the full gravity of their impact, then conceivably the quality of their overall decisions would be much different. Plainly speaking, there are those who wouldn't just let men have their way with them.

They wouldn't just give their heart, mind, and body away so easily. If this value was understood, I believe many women would be much more *selective* and less *superficial* about the men they choose to date, marry, or build a life with.

This Is Not a Competition, But a Catastrophe!

Furthermore, it appears that somehow in the rat race we find in today's society, many women have become totally consumed by the "competition" of attaining stuff and acquiring social status. In fact, some are absorbed with such a spirit of "conquest" that they are even willing to cast their moral values aside, in the name of competition. But the real question is this: if they are always in competition, whom do they feel they're in competition with? For the most part, in society, men have always been considered the "heavy weight champions." In the meantime, while many women are now entering the workplace, striving to become "number one contenders," whom are they actually fighting? Each other!

When taken from this viewpoint, one can clearly see why sisterhood or sharing knowledge and life-experiences are no longer the standard operating procedures. After all, why would they feel comfortable sharing anything with any other competitor? Right? Wrong! Where this misguided sense of competition exists, women must begin snuffing it out!

Consequently today, that is one of the main roots of dysfunction, which is hindering the quality of relationships and productivity many women are lacking in their lives, especially amongst themselves. Certainly, this is a real problem that can only be addressed by mutual trust, careful dialogue, and a deliberate, determined re-engagement amongst women.

She Is Not an Opponent, But A Sister!

You know, there is a common saying: "Behind every great man there is a strong woman!" Well, I believe it is only fitting that you begin to ask yourself, then who's behind you? Generally, as a woman, you will always find someone or something to nurture, but the real question is who's supporting, nurturing, encouraging, challenging and preparing you? A man can offer those things as well, but at the same time, no woman is an island unto herself. Aside from men, you need the healthy, social, and relational interactions with other women.

In life, you will be faced with many situations and circumstances. There will be decisions, concerns and questions you won't have all the answers to. There will be many moments where your prospective alone won't be enough. That is when you will need to look to your left and to your right to find the relationship, support and encouragement from another sister!

Certainly, I can understand some of the cynicism that exists today, but I also insist that not *every* woman is your competition.

Some of the women you know, and will meet, *may* possess a tremendous wealth of knowledge or life experience you *could* stand to learn from. These are your sisters, and they need you just as much as you will need them. Surely, life is tough enough without you endeavoring to travel its winding roads alone.

It is time to Live, Love and Learn

I hope we can agree that it's time for the warring, betrayal, and back biting to cease. Each of you is uniquely beautiful, talented, and different, so put away all of the petty and immature grievances. Are there any female relationships in your life, which needs some fixing? Don't be afraid or unwilling to mend those relationships. I urge you to remain open to the notion of making new female acquaintances. Why? Because beyond all of the warring, it's time for many women to start living, loving and even learning from one another again.

Life is a teacher

You know, the funny thing about life is that you really don't know anything until *it* teaches you something. Life itself is a *teacher* and the tools of its craft are *circumstances* and *situations*.

It is from those trials and errors of experience that we gain understanding. Wisdom, however, is measured by *what we do* with that understanding. Therefore, practical application is everything! Just imagine you have been given a private audience with Donald

Trump and he tells you every secret to becoming a millionaire. If you fail to *apply* that understanding, then there is no *reward* of wisdom, only an *empty* experience. Can you grasp what I am saying here? I hope you can because, in part, that is the underlining premise of the second half of this conversation.

How Do You Feel About Mentorship?

Right now, we're going to talk about what you are *willing* to *learn* from *others,* namely, older women. There is a point of view I want to highlight for you out of the Bible that states:

"Older women likewise are to be, teaching what is good, so that they may encourage the young women to love their husbands, to love their children, to be sensible, pure, workers at home and kind-hearted." **-Titus 2:3-5**

In a nutshell, all that's really being promoted here is the natural concept of mentoring. Have you ever been mentored? Sure, you have. Maybe you've just been unaware of it?

Ever started a new job and they put you under close supervision for a couple of weeks? They call it "training," while actually you were involved in a process of mentorship. The same goes for any promotion. A person doesn't just wake up and say one day: *"Hey I think I've been here long enough, it's time for my advancement!"* No, it usually doesn't happen like that. Generally, there are a few questions that first needs answering: "Have you been trained? Are you effective, reliable, and responsible?

Essentially, have you been mentored? You see, being mentored is all about what you are willing to learn from someone else. The kicker is whether you're teachable.

Obviously, you can now see that the idea of mentorship is more common than one would think. Education is aligned with every step of life that you take, and so we are all constantly in the process of learning and therefore being taught.

Are You Teachable?

The real questions you ought to consider are these: what am I learning? And who am I allowing to teach me? Particularly, there is an *unsafe* chasm between the classes of old and young women nowadays. Some would call it a "generational divide." This is not good, because it's not supposed to be a natural occurrence. Don't be afraid to learn from the past, particularly the past of others.

Remember, there is nothing new under the sun. There is a saying which goes, "It's better to be prepared without an opportunity than to get an opportunity and not be prepared." Why go through life experiencing things and making the *same* mistakes as many others made before you? Instead, while you have the chance, be *willing* to learn something from another person, something that you may not have to experience for yourself.

My point here is simple. You are not an island unto yourself. You need help. So essentially you must be willing to "learn from the village" in order to grow into the woman that's impacting society and the world in the way that women have always done.

Understand that in life, wisdom is not the teacher, it is the *product* of experience. Although I am not implying that older women are smarter or more intelligent than you are. I am simply suggesting that they have obviously lived longer and have had more *experiences* than you have. Therefore, due to the life they've lived and their many experiences, perhaps they've garnered wisdom as a product of those *lessons* learned.

How Deep Is Your Well?

So, when you have women who are 10, 20, 30, 40 years older than you, it's not that they're more intelligent, but that they do represent deeper well of wisdom that is a direct product of their "life experiences." Although you do share many *common* experiences as women, the underlying issue is that older women have perhaps "gone through" much of what you are *now* experiencing for the *first* time in your own personal life. Why waste 10, 20, 30, and 40 years of *your* life when you can openly reap where you have not sown and drink from wells you did not have to dig for yourself? Surely then, the "fountain of youth" isn't water that is contaminated by hast and inexperience, but rather fermented by time, wisdom and the invaluable experiences of others.

Truly, there is prudence in seeking wisdom since it's a rare product. For instance, some people are comfortable with buying a product and then there are those who are fortunate enough to have something given to them that didn't cost them a dime. Therefore, when you "receive" the wisdom of others or go to those women who possess more *experience* you're actually taking advantage of something that was "paid for" and is now being freely given to you.

Therefore, when you take such deposits and apply them to your own life experience, to a certain extent, life itself doesn't have to teach you in the same manner as others. The choice is yours! Either you can benefit from what other women have *learned* or perhaps life will take *you* through your own process only to teach you the very *same* lessons.

Find A Trusted Mentor

Now certainly, I want to be very practical in stating that wisdom itself cannot take away the "bite" of life, but it does offer us the antidotes to many of life's ills. Wisdom will not eliminate your life experiences, but it will enable you to handle yourself better in the process. Finally, as we end this conversation keep in mind that all wisdom begets a benefit. Wisdom always adds to you, it gives you something. Concerning hardship, when you "go through" it, it gives you perseverance! *Experience* then grants you the *wisdom* to know that even though you're going through challenges, that there is going to be an end.

So ultimately, the best piece of advice I want to offer is that you take the time to seek out mentorship and wisdom. Turn to your mom, auntie, sister, cousin, friend, or preferably someone older that you honor, respect, and are *willing* to *learn* from. I firmly believe that when you do this, it will greatly enrich your overall quality of life. So, choose your mentor wisely!

Made in the USA
Columbia, SC
25 September 2017